OTHER PEOPLE'S HAPPINESS

Adam Seidel

BROADWAY PLAY PUBLISHING INC
New York
www.broadwayplaypub.com
info@broadwayplaypub.com

OTHER PEOPLE'S HAPPINESS
© Copyright 2021 Adam Seidel

First edition: March 2021
I S B N: 978-0-88145-897-8

Book design: Marie Donovan
Page make-up: Adobe InDesign
Typeface: Palatino

OTHER PEOPLE'S HAPPINESS received its world premier at Playhouse on the Square in Memphis, opening 6 January 2017. The cast and creative contributors were:

SARA	Jeanna Juleson
JOHN	Gordon Ginsberg
JOEL	Standrew Parker
FRAN	Jacquelen Karel

Director	Leah Bray Nichols
Set design	Jackie Nichols
Lighting design	Mandy Heath
Sound design	Carter McHaan
Stage management	Caitlin Matthews
Wardrobe	Beth Clark

CHARACTERS & SETTING

JOHN, *late fifties. Father.*
SARA, *mid fifties. Mother.*
JOEL, *early thirties. Son.*
FRAN, *early thirties. Daughter.*

WILLIAS, CHRIS, DOCTOR, *played by one actor in his 30s.*

Time: The play takes place over the course of a year.

All settings can be and should be established with very minimal staging elements, mainly relying on lights and sound.

Scene 1

(Early summer. A small boat on a lake in the north woods. JOHN sits holding a fishing rod. Sitting behind him reading a paper is his wife, SARA. He exhales.)

SARA: What?

JOHN: What?

SARA: You exhaled.

JOHN: Did I?

SARA: So it wasn't intentional?

JOHN: Why would it be?

SARA: When you exhale, it means you have something to say.

JOHN: I don't do that. When do I do that?

SARA: At the dinner table. Which means you're looking for me to ask what's wrong.

Or when we're watching a movie you don't like.

JOHN: I suppose I do do that, don't I?

SARA: It's one of your many quirks.

JOHN: What are my other quirks?

SARA: Why?

JOHN: I'm just curious.

SARA: Would you like me to list them off?

JOHN: If you feel it's necessary.

SARA: I would prefer not to get into it.

JOHN: Do I slurp my soup? Do I sleepwalk? Do I hog the bed?

SARA: Our bed is far too big.

JOHN: Do I fart when I sleep?

SARA: I'd say that's more of an attribute than a quirk.

JOHN: Great.

SARA: You're upset.

JOHN: Not at all.

SARA: I shouldn't have said anything.

JOHN: I'm fine.

SARA: You sound irritated.

JOHN: If I sound irritated it's because you tell me I have all these quirks and when I ask what they are you pretend not to know. Wouldn't you find that irritating too?

SARA: I thought you weren't irritated.

JOHN: You know what I meant.

SARA: The only reason I said anything is because I thought you had something so say.

JOHN: And if I had something to say I'd say it.

SARA: I'm glad we cleared that up.

(They resettle into their positions.)

JOHN: But if I was going to say something—

SARA: Yes.

JOHN: It would be that, well it's silly.

SARA: What?

JOHN: You really want to know?

SARA: It's your thing to say so if you want to say it then by all means. But silence is fine too.

(*A brief pause*)

JOHN: I'm happy to be up here this weekend. That's what I wanted to say.

SARA: Really?

JOHN: Yes.

SARA: Huh.

JOHN: What?

SARA: I don't see what all the fuss was about. We can come up any time. Hop in the car and six hours later, pine trees, mosquitos, and fish galore.

JOHN: It's more than just being up here. What I'm saying is being up here with you. Just the two of us. We've both grown so busy. Me always at the office and you always at campus. We really don't see each other as much as we should. So that's why this is great.

SARA: I thought you were bored.

JOHN: Why would you think I'm bored?

SARA: You've been sitting around in your underwear.

JOHN: It's a sign of being relaxed.

SARA: When I'm relaxed I don't sit around in my underwear.

JOHN: I miss you, Sara. I miss us. What we used to have when we were younger, before we had kids and careers and responsibility. When it was just me and you and our whole lives ahead of us.

SARA: That's...nice.

JOHN: I was hoping for another reaction.

SARA: How would you like me to react?

JOHN: In a more reciprocal manner.

SARA: You want me to miss you too?

JOHN: Yes.

SARA: How can I miss you when I'm sitting next to you?

JOHN: I didn't mean in a literal sense.

SARA: Then what are you saying? That you miss me in a figurative sense? In a metaphorical sense? In a psychic sense?

JOHN: Okay Sara. Turn it into a joke.

SARA: I'm sorry, John. But you're acting very strange.

JOHN: I just feel this feeling like I'm living this life that's not mine. Like all these things around me belong together but I don't. Like I'm the lead actor in my story except someone else should be playing the part. It's eating away at me, Sara. And I have to do something about it. I'm sorry I brought any of this up.

SARA: No. It's good you did. Truthfully I feel the same way.

JOHN: You do?

SARA: I also feel like we are horribly disconnected.

JOHN: This is exactly why we needed to come up here.

SARA: Why?

JOHN: I may not always say it but I hope you know how much I love you, Sara. You mean the world to me and I'd do anything for you.

SARA: It's not that I don't think that's a sweet thing to say, because I do.

JOHN: And?

SARA: We both deserve to be happy. Right?

JOHN: Right.

SARA: And right now we aren't.

JOHN: Not at all.

SARA: So maybe the time has come for us to find happiness ourselves.

JOHN: What do you mean?...

SARA: I don't know how to say this so I'm just going to say it. I think we should split up.

JOHN: What?

SARA: I've met someone.

JOHN: I don't understand what that means.

SARA: It means I've met someone else and I want to be with them not you.

JOHN: Of all the times to throw this at me. We're fishing!

SARA: I wanted to discus it later but you brought it up.

JOHN: Who is he?

SARA: You don't know him.

JOHN: One of your students?

SARA: Please.

JOHN: Another professor?

SARA: His name is Willias. *(Will-eye-us)* He's a poet.

JOHN: A poet? You don't even like poetry.

SARA: I do now.

JOHN: This is completely irrational.

SARA: But I'm happy.

JOHN: That doesn't mean you should go off and fire bomb everything you have.

SARA: But everything I have makes me miserable.

JOHN: Then approach what you have from another angle and try to re-embrace it.

SARA: That's delusional!

JOHN: It's pragmatic!

SARA: John I'm leaving you.

JOHN: You can't.

SARA: Why not?

JOHN: You're a professor. You have a family. You have responsibilities. Soon enough you'll be a grandmother. And you'll retire and so will I and we'll spend our golden years traveling the world seeing all the sights we've always wanted to see.

SARA: Willias and I have decided to move in together.

JOHN: You're moving out?

SARA: Actually he's moving in. That being said I'd like the house in the city.

JOHN: You can't have the house.

SARA: It's not an unreasonable request. Especially since you don't even like it.

JOHN: I built that house!

SARA: Your brother built it.

JOHN: I hired him!

SARA: Which is something I never understood. He's a lousy architect.

JOHN: Can we just slow down for a minute?

SARA: How?

JOHN: For the past three hours we've been fishing in complete peace and quiet and now all of a sudden we're talking about who gets what and who's doing who and before this goes any further you should stop and think about this.

SARA: I've been thinking about this, John.

JOHN: I know how your mind works. And you're more rational than this.

SARA: Rational.

JOHN: I mean look at us, Sara. Look at our life. Sure it's not perfect, but who's is? Now I'm not happy about this thing you're doing. And we'll need to have further conversations about that. But the bottom line is I love you. I want us to spend the rest of our lives together and I'm willing to do what it takes to make that happen.

SARA: Do you want the Volvo or the Land Cruiser?

JOHN: Sara I don't want a divorce.

SARA: Then we don't have to get one. But I'm not going to stop.

JOHN: I've always tried to be there for you. What more do you want?

SARA: I want more EVERYTHING. I want to wake up in the morning and be excited. I want to feel adventure. I want to have thrills. And terror. And fright. And you know what? I want more sex too. I mean Jesus, you're like a monk.

JOHN: I'm finished talking about this!

SARA: Sorry if it stings but the only thing that reaches you is brutal honesty.

JOHN: Aren't you forgetting something? The kids.

SARA: What about them?

JOHN: This is going to be tough on them.

SARA: Good.

JOHN: How is that good?

SARA: They've never had to confront anything truly difficult.

JOHN: Our kids were raised to understand the value of things.

SARA: They've been given a false sense of security and it's time they learned the ultimate lesson— Life's a bitch. The sooner they learn that the better.

(*A moment of digestion*)

JOHN: I'll spend a few weeks up here. And when you realize the mistake you're making I'll come back and we can deal with this like rational adults.

SARA: You are so principled. It's the one thing I've always admired.

(SARA *goes back to her book. They sit in silence.*)

Scene 2

(*A week later. The family company.* FRAN *in her office looking over a report.* JOEL *enters.*)

JOEL: Fran.

FRAN: Joel.

JOEL: You look tired.

FRAN: The past week I've been running this place myself.

JOEL: Where's dad?

FRAN: At the cabin.

JOEL: I thought him and mom were just going for the weekend.

FRAN: Well he decided to stay longer. Now what can I do for you?

JOEL: Do you know of anything going on at the house?

FRAN: What would be going on at the house?

JOEL: I don't know but I drove by yesterday and there was this beat up Toyota in the driveway. Then today the car was still there and this shirtless dude was carrying boxes in the house.

FRAN: Why are you driving by the house?

JOEL: I'm not allowed to drive by the house?

FRAN: It's no where near where you live.

JOEL: So you don't think some dude moving boxes into the house is weird?

FRAN: Joel I'm really busy here so whatever you're getting at just get at it.

JOEL: I'd like to go check things out and I want you to come.

FRAN: Even if I wanted to, which I don't, I can't because I have like fifteen more calls to make by lunch. Send mom my regards.

JOEL: I'm nervous to go over there alone.

FRAN: Why?

JOEL: I haven't talked to mom in a week.

FRAN: She hasn't called?

JOEL: No.

FRAN: Try calling her?

JOEL: She doesn't pick up.

FRAN: Maybe a little time apart from her will do you good.

JOEL: You spend way more time with dad than I do with mom.

FRAN: We work together so I'd say it's a little different.

JOEL: Look. I'm asking you, as my big sister, who I never ask for favors, to please do this with me, because dad's paintings are on the lawn and it's super weird.

FRAN: What do you mean his paintings are on the lawn?

JOEL: Just what I said. When I drove by his paintings were on the lawn along with his clothes.

(A beat)

FRAN: I'll get my coat.

(FRAN *and* JOEL *exit.)*

Scene 3

(Later that day. In the back yard of the family house in the city. SARA is dressed in blue and white striped yoga pants and a tank top sitting on a yoga mat very still. Her eyes are closed and she meditates. Really stereotypical Indian meditation music plays from a portable boom box.)

(FRAN *enters. Then* JOEL. *They look at* SARA.*)*

FRAN: Mom.

(Nothing from SARA*)*

JOEL: Mom?

(Nothing from SARA*)*

FRAN: MOM.

(SARA *calmly opens her eyes, seeing them.)*

SARA: Fran. Joel. What a surprise!

JOEL: What are you doing?

SARA: Yoga. It's funny— When I used to walk past yoga places I'd always roll my eyes, but I have to say it's a really wonderful way to exercise. Especially doing it out here in the back yard. The grass. The sun. The sky. All these trees, the way their branches dance in the wind. It's just heavenly. It's never too late to try new things.

(SARA *goes into a pose. She's a beginner so all the poses she does are beginner level and should not look ridiculous or stupid.*)

FRAN: Speaking of new things, you mind telling us what the hell's going on?

SARA: In what sense honey?

FRAN: In the sense that dad's stuff is all over the front lawn, the hall's full of moving boxes and there's some guy frying dough in the kitchen?

SARA: Well, your father's things are on the front lawn because your father no longer lives here. And the boxes in the hall belong to Willias, who's frying feta, not dough.

JOEL: And who exactly is Willias?

SARA: I suppose one could call him my boyfriend.

JOEL: As in he's a boy who's a friend?

SARA: Yes. And we're dating. Any other questions?

JOEL: For the moment I'm just processing.

SARA: Great. (*She goes into another pose.*)

FRAN: I'm sorry, does dad know about any of this?

SARA: Of course.

FRAN: And how does he feel about it?

SARA: I don't know. I haven't asked for his input. Now look, if you could give me ten minutes, we can discuss everything after yoga. (*She goes into another pose.*)

FRAN: Great. So mom's gone off the reservation.

JOEL: Whoa.

FRAN: What?

JOEL: That's racist.

FRAN: Okay relax.

JOEL: No I will not relax. Native Americans were horrifically removed from their lands by force and making jest of it—

SARA: I haven't gone off the reservation. I've just decided it's time be honest about what I really want.

FRAN: Which is what, mom?

SARA: To be not married to your father anymore.

JOEL: Okay excuse me?

SARA: At the cabin last weekend your father and I had a very honest discussion, and I asked him for a divorce.

JOEL: A divorce??

SARA: I know that's quite sudden and I don't want to shock you.

JOEL: Too late. I'm shocked. Very shocked.

(A guy with an unbuttoned shirt and shorts enters, WILLIAS. He's got a very positive attitude.)

WILLIAS: Okay! Feta is fried and lunch is served! Hey you must be Fran and Joel!

FRAN: Uh huh.

JOEL: Uh huh.

WILLIAS: I've heard so much about you both! I'm Willias!

(WILLIAS extends his hand first to FRAN who just looks at him. Then he extends it to JOEL who gives him an awkward limp handshake.)

WILLIAS: I'm picking up on weird energy, so maybe this was a bad time to come out.

FRAN: Actually it was the perfect time because we're leaving.

SARA: Don't. Stay for lunch and we'll talk things over like adults.

FRAN: We don't need to talk because I only have one thing to say- Whatever this is, you're not getting away with it. So stop now.

(FRAN *exits.*)

SARA: She gets very angry, doesn't she? *(Looking at* JOEL.*)* Honey have you done something new with your hair?

JOEL: No?

SARA: *(Genuinely complimenting him.)* It looks nice.

JOEL: We'll talk later.

WILLIAS: Nice to meet you man!

JOEL: You too?

(JOEL *exits.* SARA *gets up, rolls up her mat and her and* WILLIAS *exit the opposite way.)*

Scene 4

(A week later. An outside porch at the cabin in the northwoods. JOHN *is sitting at an outdoor table with* FRAN *and* JOEL. *All three have plates of food. Both* FRAN *and* JOEL *are watching* JOHN. JOHN *realizes they are looking at him.)*

JOHN: How's the food?

JOEL: It's great dad.

JOHN: Fran you haven't have touched your plate.

FRAN: I'm not hungry.

JOEL: The corn is amazing. How do you give it that flavor?

JOHN: A little paprika. Little sea salt. Lots of butter.

JOEL: That's what it is. Paprika.

FRAN: He's made the corn the same damn way for thirty years.

JOEL: She's just tired from the drive.

FRAN: I'm not tired from the drive.

JOEL: We're both tired from the drive.

JOHN: Pass the salt.

(JOEL *passes the salt.*)

FRAN: Dad you can't hide up here forever!

JOEL: Fran.

FRAN: I know we're supposed to be pretending everything is fine but I can't.

JOHN: I'm not hiding.

FRAN: Then what are you doing?

JOEL: He's resting.

FRAN: Dad can answer for himself.

JOHN: I'm resting.

FRAN: Resting is taking the day off or spending a night in. But living out here in the middle of nowhere for two weeks is hiding.

JOEL: Leave it alone, Fran.

FRAN: I'm concerned about dad.

JOEL: So am I.

FRAN: Then stop acting like everything is normal.

JOHN: Listen, I appreciate you two coming up, but you really didn't have to.

JOEL: *(Re-assuring)* I know dad.

JOHN: I mean, everything is fine.

JOEL: *(More re-assuring)* Of course it is.

FRAN: Dad, do you even know what's going on?

JOHN: In what sense?

FRAN: With mom.

JOHN: We're going through a rough patch.

JOEL: And that's perfectly normal for any heathy relationship. Take James and me. Last year with his career taking off, meanwhile my work being ignored? But, we communicated our feelings, and now our relationship is stronger than ever.

JOHN: Pass the rolls.

(JOEL *passes the rolls.*)

FRAN: Have you talked to mom?

JOHN: No.

FRAN: Well you should because she's gone off the—

JOEL: Don't say reservation.

FRAN: I was going to say "rails", P C police.

JOEL: She hasn't gone off the rails, mom's just expressing new found freedom caused by disassociating with her identity. I've been reading some books on the "three quarter life crises". All this stuff is very common. The kids leave the nest, there's a void and to fill that void people sometimes take drastic measures.

FRAN: As in asking for a divorce and having some Greek yoga bro move in to the house?

JOEL: His name is Willias and no one is getting a divorce. Because this is temporary.

JOHN: Do we have any rye bread?

JOEL: I think there's some in the cupboard. *(He gets up)* I'll be right back. *(To* FRAN*)* Behave. *(He exits.)*

FRAN: Look. I know this isn't what you want to hear, but you need to come back.

JOHN: Why.

FRAN: Because you have to.

JOHN: Why.

FRAN: For the company.

JOHN: You run the company.

FRAN: Then how about for your dignity?

JOHN: I have plenty of dignity.

FRAN: Listen. No one thinks any less of you. People admire you for sticking it out with mom as long as you did.

JOHN: What does that mean?

FRAN: It's no big secret that you two weren't getting along. I'm not saying you need to reconcile. But you can't stay this defeated man. It's beneath you.

JOHN: Can we please discuss something else?

FRAN: Like what?

JOHN: The weather.

FRAN: I hate talking about the weather.

JOHN: Then pick another subject!

(JOEL *enters with loaf of rye bread.*)

JOEL: Rye bread!

JOHN: Wonderful.

FRAN: Listen. I get where you're coming from. And I can't imagine how hard this is on you. But things back home have descended into chaos and you need to restore order.

JOEL: I'd hardly call this situation chaos. Politics in Africa? Now that's chaos.

FRAN: Mom's living with some guy and her and dad aren't divorced.

JOEL: And no one is getting a divorce.

FRAN: Given the situation that's where things seem to be headed.

JOEL: Not like dad's been served.

FRAN: How do you know?

JOEL: He would have told us. Right dad?

JOHN: Someone pass the butter.

FRAN: Whether or not he's been served doesn't matter. It's inevitable one day he'll be sitting up here and get a tap on the shoulder and it'll be the Sheriff serving him with papers.

JOHN: The butter please?

JOEL: Sheriff's don't serve papers, a process server does. And none of this even matters because no one is getting divorced!

(JOHN *pounds his fist on the table.*)

JOHN: Will someone pass the goddamn butter?!

(Silence. JOEL *passes the butter.)*

JOHN: Look. I was going to wait till later but I might as well tell you now. The day before last I was served.

JOEL: What?

JOHN: And I've decided I'm going to sign.

JOEL: Dad.

JOHN: I know this is hard to understand, Joel. But since I've been up here I've come to realize this life isn't what I want so I'm giving it up.

JOEL: We all know mom is being extremely difficult right now, but without her you will crumble. I know it. You know it. The whole world knows it!

JOHN: I've made up my mind, Joel. It's final.

JOEL: So now that it's, as you say, final, what are you going to do?

JOHN: Honestly? I was thinking of starting a restaurant. Not too many restaurants in these parts.

JOEL: Because we're in the middle of nowhere! *(Rebooting the positivity.)* I didn't want to get into this now but before coming up here I did some research and you two can go to a marriage counseling retreat.

JOHN: Joel...

(JOEL takes several folded up pamphlets out of his pocket.)

JOEL: There's Mended Fences in Waukegan *(Wa-key-gan)* which is pretty standard. There's Rekindled Embers in Glen Ellen which is first rate. But my personal favorite is Soul Doves in Lake Geneva. "Just because your love flies away doesn't mean it can't return to the coop."

JOHN: Joel, you have to realize when the party is over. And it's over.

JOEL: Fran? Free to jump in at any time.

FRAN: I'm glad you're divorcing her, dad. Ef her.

JOEL: Take that back.

FRAN: Ef mom and her greek yoga boyfriend!

JOEL: If you were going to start with the doom and gloom why'd you even come up here?

FRAN: Because I knew you were going to pump dad's head full of this bull shit.

JOEL: I'm trying to save our family from total meltdown!

FRAN: You can't save it Joel. Because no matter what you do, nothing will change the fact that mom's an asshole.

JOEL: I'm done listening to you.

FRAN: Asshole!

JOEL: I'm sorry did someone say something?!

FRAN: Assholeassholeasshole—

JOEL: LALALALALALALALALA.

JOHN: AHHHHHHHH!!!!!! *(Silence)* I'm tired. Tired of the nagging. Tired of stress, tired of confusion and most importantly, I'm tired of fighting. I want peace and quiet and if you can't respect that then pack up and get out.

FRAN: Maybe we should go inside.

JOEL: I think that's a good idea. What do you say dad? Feel like going inside?

JOHN: Do you hear that?

FRAN: Hear what?

JOHN: That bird off in the distance. I think it's a loon.

FRAN: I don't hear anything.

JOHN: Loons are regarded as a symbol of harmony and peace, which has always struck me as strange. Their call has such a sad, piercing tone. Once you hear that sound you never forget it.

JOEL: You okay, dad?

JOHN: Shhh. There it is again. *(He stares off into the distance.)*

Scene 5

(A few weeks later. In JOEL's *art studio.* JOEL *stands with* SARA. *She's looking at a strange sculpture that resembles a goat.* JOEL *is observing her.)*

JOEL: So?

SARA: Give me a moment.

JOEL: Keep in mind it's not finished. I still have tweaks I'd like to do.

SARA: You're defending before you know what I think.

JOEL: You've been staring at it for five minutes.

SARA: I'll take it.

JOEL: Tell me what you like about it.

SARA: Well. The angles are intriguing. The proportions are very nice. Plus I've always liked goats.

JOEL: It's a dog.

SARA: It's got horns.

JOEL: The horns are a metaphor. Man's best friend but not really?

SARA: Oh. I thought the whole thing was a Cubs reference.

JOEL: Just forget it.

SARA: I still want it.

JOEL: Mom—

SARA: Don't argue. Just tell me how much.

JOEL: I was gonna ask a thousand.

SARA: I'll give you twelve hundred. *(Pause)* Going once. Going twice.

JOEL: Okay.

SARA: Great. It's a wonderful piece. Your work is really coming along.

JOEL: Glad someone thinks so.

SARA: I know what I'm looking at.

JOEL: I know you have a good eye. But I haven't sold anything in a few months. And galleries don't seem to be interested.

SARA: Have patience. Look at Van Gogh. His audience didn't find him until he was dead.

JOEL: If this is your attempt at a motivation speech it's not working.

SARA: Then how's this? Keep sculpting or get a desk job.

JOEL: Technically sculpting is a desk job cause when I do it I sit at my desk. But point taken.

SARA: How is James doing?

JOEL: He's good. Busy. Sends hugs and kisses.

SARA: And how are you two doing?

JOEL: We're really...good.

SARA: You trying to convince me or yourself?

JOEL: We're still going through some turbulence.

SARA: Feel like talking about it?

JOEL: You don't want to know.

SARA: I do or I wouldn't have asked.

JOEL: Okay so there's this curator in Paris that he's been talking with for a few months and yesterday he got word that she's giving him a solo show.

SARA: Well that's great.

JOEL: Yeah except my reaction wasn't exactly enthusiastic and that pissed him off which pissed me off and then he grabbed his backpack and left.

SARA: I'm sorry.

JOEL: Eh it'll be fine. Just need to give it a few days. Besides nothing like a good row to stir up inspiration.

SARA: I was nervous about seeing you today.

JOEL: You don't get nervous.

SARA: Which made me more nervous. We haven't spoken for almost two weeks, and part of me thought maybe you'd disowned me.

JOEL: I'd never disown you. I mean, who'd buy my art? Kidding. I was nervous too. Not seeing you has been, tough.

SARA: I should have reached out sooner.

JOEL: It's probably best you didn't. I needed time to figure out how I felt about, everything.

SARA: How do you feel about everything? If it's too much we don't have to—

JOEL: No it's fine I'm good to dive in. So here it goes- I'd of preferred other courses of action were taken, like any other course, really. But when it comes down to it, if you felt like you needed to make a change, who am I to say you can't?

SARA: Well. That's quite mature.

JOEL: I've been reading lots of Eastern Philosophy.

SARA: So you're okay with things?

JOEL: I don't think I'd use the word 'okay'. But if we can all find a way to be civil, and that includes us continuing to celebrate holidays together as a family minus the jarringly positive yoga guy, I can accept your divorce.

SARA: Your father and I aren't divorced yet.

JOEL: No?

SARA: Which is something I wanted to talk to you about.

JOEL: Please tell me you're not thinking of marrying this other guy.

SARA: Of course not. What I was going to say is your father reached out.

JOEL: He called you?

SARA: He emailed.

JOEL: I didn't know there was internet at the cabin.

SARA: I don't know, I guess he had it installed. At any rate he told me that before he agrees to sign any papers, he wants me to come up to the cabin so we can speak in person. And the fact is, I just can't go up there right now.

JOEL: Not to take dad's side, but don't you think you owe him that?

SARA: I'm not disagreeing, but I've got things going on I can't get away from.

JOEL: Like what?

SARA: Things which are my business that I'm not going to discuss. Anyway, I wanted to ask if you'd go in my place.

JOEL: Mom—

SARA: And you can see what he wants and then tell me.

JOEL: Mom.

SARA: I know it's a lot to ask.

JOEL: You buying my art is a lot to ask. But asking me go up to the cabin to be your mediator or whatever isÉ Wait, you didn't buy the sculpture as a bribe, did you?

SARA: What?

JOEL: Oh my God you totally did.

SARA: Of course I didn't. I bought the piece because I believe in you. I just really need you to do this for me. Please.

JOEL: I suppose I could go up this weekend.

SARA: Thank you.

JOEL: But I want you to buy my gas which is like seventy bucks round trip.

SARA: Done.

JOEL: And I want additional money for food.

SARA: How much?

JOEL: A hundred on top of the gas.

SARA: You can take it out of the twelve hundred I just paid you.

(Beat)

JOEL: Should I tell Fran I'm doing this?

SARA: Do you think that's a good idea?

JOEL: She'll get pissed if I don't.

SARA: She'll get pissed no matter what.

JOEL: Maybe it's best she doesn't know.

SARA: I think that's wise.

(Lights fade.)

Scene 6

(Later same week. FRAN's place. She stands with her husband CHRIS, who wears a suit.)

FRAN: This is not a fight.

CHRIS: So what is it?

FRAN: We're talking. This is how we talk.

CHRIS: Blowing up at me over some dirty dishes in the sink as I'm headed out the door is not talking.

FRAN: I don't care about the dishes.

CHRIS: Then what? Is this about your mom and dad?

FRAN: No.

CHRIS: It's okay if it is.

FRAN: It's not.

CHRIS: Then what?! Come on. Talk to me. What was the point of all that couples therapy if we're not communicating?

FRAN: I feel like I barely see you.

CHRIS: That's what this is about?

FRAN: Lately you're gone all the time.

CHRIS: Well, not all the time.

FRAN: Enough of the time that it really bothers me. Especially right now.

CHRIS: You mean with your parents.

FRAN: Yes.

CHRIS: I thought you said that wasn't bothering you?

FRAN: I'm just having a lot of thoughts right now.

CHRIS: I'm sorry I've been gone. But you know my job involves traveling, and this quarter has been super crazy, and not to deflect, but ever since you took the helm over at the family biz you work all the time too.

FRAN: I know.

CHRIS: So then what are we even talking about?

FRAN: Sometimes it feels like when you're here you're not.

CHRIS: I don't know what that means.

(FRAN *builds up the courage, then dives in.*)

FRAN: Are you seeing her again?

CHRIS: What.

FRAN: Are you?

CHRIS: Fran.

FRAN: Or maybe you're not seeing her but you're seeing someone else.

CHRIS: I've told you a million times, that's over with.

FRAN: Then who were you texting?

CHRIS: When?

FRAN: The other night. I walked in the bedroom and you were sitting there texting, and when you saw me you put your phone down.

CHRIS: Oh. Wow. I put the phone down.

FRAN: It was the way you did it. Like you were hiding something.

CHRIS: I don't have time to get into this.

FRAN: So I didn't catch you off guard?

CHRIS: Have things gotten to the point where I can't do anything without you assuming the worst?

FRAN: Who were you texting??

CHRIS: I don't remember.

FRAN: That is such crap!

CHRIS: I don't! But you wanna see my phone? Here.

(CHRIS *holds out his phone.* FRAN *doesn't take it.*)

CHRIS: Come on. Look at it.

FRAN: Looking at your phone proves nothing because you're not dumb enough to not erase a text.

CHRIS: You're really nuts, you know that?? (*He puts the phone away.*)

FRAN: So now I'm nuts.

CHRIS: You're acting nuts.

FRAN: So you're telling me I'm wrong?

CHRIS: I've done nothing to make you suspicious.

FRAN: Except that you were boinking a stewardess from Texas.

CHRIS: Flight attendant.

FRAN: You're really gonna make that distinction???

CHRIS: I feel like no matter what I do you're never going to trust me again.

FRAN: I want to.

CHRIS: Well, I don't think it's going to happen. So maybe we should just end it.

FRAN: What?

CHRIS: I'm just saying.

FRAN: Is that what you want?

CHRIS: It seems like it's what you want.

FRAN: No I don't want that.

CHRIS: Then why are you pushing me away?

FRAN: I'm not trying to. It's just, I'm having a really hard time with everything going on and I don't know…maybe I'm seeing things that aren't there.

CHRIS: Look, can we pick this up when I get back? If I don't leave right now I'm gonna miss this flight.

FRAN: Yeah. Sure.

CHRIS: Great. See you Thursday, okay? Okay?

FRAN: Okay.

(CHRIS *kisses* FRAN. *He exits. She watches him a moment, then exits the other way.*)

Scene 7

*(The weekend. A wooden handmade bench in a clearing
in the north woods.* JOHN *enters, now dressed in a flannel
shirt.)*

JOHN: Found it!

JOEL: *(Off)* Where are you?

JOHN: Over here!

JOEL: *(Off)* Where?

JOHN: Here.

(After a moment JOEL *enters, also dressed in a flannel shirt.)*

JOEL: I remember it being bigger.

JOHN: We built it when you were little. You remember?

JOEL: After that big storm.

JOHN: We walked out here and there it was, a giant
fallen tree. I got the saw, we went to it. *(He sits.)*

JOEL: How's it sit?

JOHN: Little bit of a tilt. But not bad. Time taking it's
toll. Nice out here isn't it?

JOEL: It's peaceful.

JOHN: Look at that lake. Not a ripple. Hey you
remember the first time we went fishing?

JOEL: You mean the only time?

JOHN: I woke you at dawn, told you to get your coat
and soon enough we were out on the lake, daylight
barely touching the tops of the trees. We were out
there hours without a bite, you begging me to head
into shore. But I said we were staying. That the key
to fishing is patience. Then you got a bite. It was a big
fish. I remember how scared you were; eyes wide,
gripping the rod so tightly your knuckles were white.
You started to reel him in. When we saw the fish's

shadow under the boat I got out the net and told you to give the reel one more crank and just as we were about to bring him in—

JOEL: The line broke and he got away.

JOHN: That was a real shame. I don't know that I've seen a bigger fish.

JOEL: Fish get away.

JOHN: I read an article in the trib about James' new exhibition. It appears to be well received. The critic used the term "fundamentally jarring". I assume that means 'good'.

JOEL: It's definitely creating a stir. He used cow blood instead of paint.

JOHN: Didn't mention that in the article.

JOEL: Probably didn't wanna piss off PETA. Though James would gladly embrace the controversy.

JOHN: I'd think the paintings would start to smell after a while.

JOEL: He varnishes them after the blood dries. Locks in all that stink.

JOHN: Speaking of, I take it your mother sent you as her bag man.

JOEL: She just had something she couldn't get away from.

JOHN: What a chicken shit.

JOEL: Okay keep in mind we're still talking about my mom. And for the record I'm not a bag man. I'm a, facilitator.

JOHN: I don't need a facilitator. I need a face to face with your mother.

JOEL: Well, she's not here, I am. So we gonna do this or what?

JOHN: Fine. Sure. Lets talk.

JOEL: Okay. Great. So what did you want to say?

JOHN: Sorry, am I talking to you as you, or as mom?

JOEL: You can just talk to me as me.

JOHN: Alright. It's just I sorta mentally prepared this whole thing talking to her, but hey, I'm adaptable.

JOEL: Glad to hear it.

JOHN: Okay, so the fact is I've had some time up here to process all that's happened. And I'll be able to move on with my post married life in a productive manner.

JOEL: Which you told Fran and I last time we came up here.

JOHN: I know. See? This is why I wanted to talk to your mom.

JOEL: Lets just skip to the thing you want.

JOHN: Before I sign any papers I need closure. And to get closure I need two things to happen. The first is I'd like an apology, which isn't going to happen since your mother isn't here, so I guess that will have to wait.

JOEL: And second?

JOHN: The city house needs to be sold.

JOEL: What do you mean?

JOHN: I mean I want that house sold. As soon as possible.

JOEL: Dad...

JOHN: I'm no longer living in the city. You and Fran are adults on your own. What person needs three bathrooms, a four car garage and a back yard the size of a forest preserve?

JOEL: Okay clearly this is a move to hurt mom.

JOHN: It has nothing to do with her.

JOEL: She's living there.

JOHN: Doesn't matter. It's not her house.

JOEL: The house is marital property which means it is.

JOHN: See, again this is where it would've been so much easier if she'd of just come up herself because she would've already understood.

JOEL: What are you talking about?

JOHN: For reasons of liability, many years ago the house was put in a living trust. The House Trust. That way if something bad ever happened with the company—

JOEL: Yes thanks I know how a trust works.

JOHN: Well, seeing how the grantor and sole trustee of The House Trust is me, that means by definition of the law if I say we're selling, we're selling.

JOEL: And if mom fights you which she surely will?

JOHN: I got nothing but lawyers and time.

JOEL: What mom's done is bad and you have every reason to be upset. But selling the house is not going to make you feel better.

JOHN: Why do you even care if I sell the house? It's not that great of a place.

JOEL: It represents my childhood. It holds memories. I walk in the living room and I see us having movie nights. I go in the kitchen and I look at the burned wallpaper next to the sink and I remember the toaster bursting into flames from a stuck piece of toast. I go into my bedroom and I see myself as a happy little kid who looked at the world as a place to explore and discover. Dad. I'm asking as your son. Please don't sell the house.

JOHN: I gave you everything you ever wanted. Supported you to no end. I thought I was helping. But all I did was give you was a sense of entitlement. I've made up my mind and I'm moving on.

JOEL: I don't know why I'm worked up about this. It's not like it matters cause the whole place is completely outdated. You'll never get a decent offer. In this market especially.

JOHN: I agree. That's why I'm having it demolished.

JOEL: What.

JOHN: The lot's worth twenty percent more without a structure on it. So bash it, burn it, trash it. I don't care, it's coming down.

JOEL: Listen to me. These are not rational thoughts.

JOHN: Probably not.

JOEL: You want revenge on mom then go in there and turn off the power. Tear out the windows. Set the lawn on fire! But having the house torn down is completely crazy!

JOHN: I don't give a shit it's what I want!!!

(A beat)

JOEL: I feel like my life is a lie.

JOHN: Relax. It's just a house.

JOEL: I'm not talking about the house, I'm talking about James' first international show.

JOHN: James is having an international show?

JOEL: In Paris.

JOHN: That's impressive.

JOEL: No, actually it's horrific. Cause I can't keep pretending we're equals. He's succeeding. I'm failing.

JOHN: Things don't always turn out like you want them to. But you're lucky enough to be in a position where you can afford to do what you want and this is the life you've chosen.

JOEL: Okay I'm not looking for life advice right now. Especially from a guy who's entire marriage was a sham.

JOHN: Our marriage was not a sham.

JOEL: You guys didn't love each other.

JOHN: I loved you mother deeply. But she stopped loving me.

JOEL: When?

JOHN: It's not important.

JOEL: Jesus Christ just give me a straight answer!

JOHN: It was right after you were born. I came into her hospital room and she was in bed holding you. The look on her face was angelic. She hadn't heard me come in so I cleared my throat. She looked up at me, and her eyes went dead. We never spoke about that moment.

JOEL: If you knew that then why did you stay? To prove you could gut it out? That you were stronger than her?

JOHN: I stayed for you and Fran. For our family. I'm sorry I shouldn't have told you that.

JOEL: Why?

JOHN: Because you're sensitive. You get overly affected by things.

JOEL: Because I'm gay?

JOHN: That's not what I meant.

JOEL: That's what it sounded like.

JOHN: I've known you were gay since you were five! I didn't care then and I don't care now!

JOEL: Honestly dad I'm glad you told me all this. Cause now I know there's someone worse off than me.

JOHN: Joel what do you want?

JOEL: I want you to stop all of this.

JOHN: I can't do that.

JOEL: You mean you won't.

JOHN: Things have gone too far.

JOEL: Great. Then go ahead and tear down the house but it's not going to do anything. Mom's happy. She smiles again. I hardly recognize her she's so happy. And there's nothing you can do to change that.

JOHN: Next time you see your mother tell her to have a ball while she can because tearing the house down is only the first step. I'm going to sell the cars and give away the art. And then I'm going to freeze the bank account. And then she'll be free to do whatever she wants with who she wants. For all I care she can rot in hell!

JOEL: I'm ashamed to be your son. *(He angrily exits.)*

JOHN: Joel. Joel! *(He looks around at his settings. He looks like he's lost.)*

Scene 8

(The house in the city. In the living room. There's an open moving box on floor along with a few old newspapers and a chair. FRAN stands on the phone.)

FRAN: *(Into phone)* Hey, haven't heard from you but I know you're really busy with stuff so I thought I'd check in. Just want you to know I'm proud of you and I hope you get the account because you deserve it. Look, can you please call me? Anytime is fine, just call?

(JOEL, *who's holding glasses, enters.* FRAN *senses his presence and her tone changes.*)

FRAN: Yeah great so anyway, love you talk soon bye. (*She hangs up.*)

JOEL: So where's old Chrissy-boy this week?

FRAN: Reno.

JOEL: Reno, Nevada. The littlest big city in the world.

FRAN: I think it's the other way around.

JOEL: He sure does travel a lot doesn't he?

FRAN: It's part of his job.

JOEL: Anyway, this is the last of the kitchen.

FRAN: Great.

JOEL: Seen mom's new place?

FRAN: Nope.

JOEL: You should. It's nice. Not as big as this place, obviously, but it's got lots of charm. Plus the building's full of kids.

FRAN: Should be great for mom as she's acting like one.

JOEL: At least she's not destroying our childhood home.

FRAN: I'm glad it's coming down.

JOEL: Fran I know it was hard for you to come here but can you try to be positive?

FRAN: Talk to dad lately?

JOEL: Not since visiting him.

FRAN: You mean when you were acting as mom's secret agent?

JOEL: I don't want to talk about it.

FRAN: So when does James leave for Paris?

JOEL: Don't want to talk about that either.

FRAN: I'll bet he's so excited.

JOEL: Let's just finish packing.

(JOEL *hands* FRAN *the glasses.* FRAN *wraps the glasses in newspaper and puts them into the box.*)

JOEL: Those don't go in there.

FRAN: What do you mean?

JOEL: That box is for plates.

FRAN: I thought we were putting everything together.

JOEL: If you put the plates in with the glasses they'll hit against each other and break.

FRAN: The glasses are wrapped with newspaper.

JOEL: Newspaper isn't going to do anything if the U-Haul hits a pothole.

FRAN: So don't drive the U-Haul over a pothole.

(JOEL *goes to the box and starts to unpack it.*)

FRAN: Joel it's fine just leave it alone.

(JOEL *ignores* FRAN.)

(FRAN *forcefully slaps* JOEL's *hand.*)

JOEL: What the heck was that?!

FRAN: Don't touch the box!!

(SARA *enters.*)

SARA: Hey what is going on out here with all the yelling??

JOEL: Fran packed the glasses with the plates.

SARA: And?

JOEL: You're not supposed to.

SARA: Just leave them the way they are.

JOEL: Fine. But when all the plates are broken…

SARA: I never realized how dark it is in here.

JOEL: It's not that dark.

SARA: It seems like someone just turned off the lights.

FRAN: The lights were never on.

SARA: It's been a big day. I think it's catching up with me.

JOEL: Sit down a sec and rest. Can I get you some water?

SARA: That'd be great.

JOEL: I'll be right back.

(JOEL *looks at* FRAN *to see if she's going to verbally attack mom in his absence. She looks at him like "What the fuck are you looking at me for?")*

(JOEL *exits. There's an awkward silence between* FRAN *and* SARA.)

SARA: How's it going?

FRAN: Almost finished packing.

SARA: I meant with you.

FRAN: I'm, great.

SARA: Good. And Chris?

FRAN: Chris is great.

SARA: Happy to hear it. *(An awkward silence)* I'm doing fine, in case you were wondering.

FRAN: You seem a bit low on energy today.

SARA: I suppose I'm tired.

FRAN: Out clubbing all night with what's his name?

SARA: Actually I haven't been sleeping well.

FRAN: They make pills for that.

SARA: I've never liked pills.

FRAN: They make pills for that too.

SARA: I want you to know I really appreciate you helping today.

FRAN: Just don't want to see dad's things get hurt.

SARA: Well I'm sure dad's things appreciate that. *(Beat)* It's strange knowing this place will be gone.

FRAN: Why?

SARA: So many cherished memories. I remember when you were a little girl we bought you that huge doll house. It was beautiful. A miniature version of a Victorian mansion, or something.

FRAN: It was tudor.

SARA: For years you loved that house. Then you became a teenager and your father decided it was time to sell it. But you had other plans. I'll never forget his face when he came home to see the doll house in the front yard, set on fire. In front of it, a little note. "If I can't have it no one else will."

FRAN: Me setting my dollhouse on fire is your cherished memory?

SARA: It certainly was memorable.

FRAN: I'm gonna see if everything is done upstairs.

SARA: Fran, I'm trying to talk to you.

FRAN: Well I don't want to talk to you. I mean what? You thought cause I came over that everything would suddenly be normal?

SARA: No. But I thought it would give us a chance to spend time together.

FRAN: Why would we spend time together?

SARA: Maybe because I haven't seen you in months.

FRAN: Because I don't want to see you.

SARA: You're mad. Good. Let loose. Let me have it.

FRAN: My life is exhausting enough.

SARA: What did Chris do now?

FRAN: What about me saying I'm exhausted automatically makes you go there?

SARA: So things between you and Chris are hunky dory?

FRAN: I'm not discussing it.

SARA: I don't understand you. How with certain things you let yourself get so trampled.

FRAN: Okay right now you need to back off!

SARA: I just mean that you're strong. Stronger than me. You're not afraid to tell people what you think.

FRAN: Neither are you.

SARA: Maybe not anymore. But for years the thought of saying something people might dislike terrified me so I'd just go along with things. Like that dog we had when you were little. What was his name? Petey? Peaches?

FRAN: Pepper.

SARA: That dog was very dumb. I don't even think he knew his name. I didn't want to get him. But your father insisted. Said getting a dog was good for children. But then he became my responsibility. I fed him. I walked him. I cleaned up after him. Then one day I accidentally left the front door open, and he got hit by a car.

FRAN: Pepper got hit by a car?

SARA: You knew that.

FRAN: You told us he ran away. Jesus mom.

SARA: The point is the whole thing could have been avoided if I'd put my foot down.

FRAN: Well congrats on finally finding your voice.

SARA: I want to know where this comes from.

FRAN: What?

SARA: The chip on your shoulder.

FRAN: It's not a chip.

SARA: Is it that you resent me?

FRAN: No.

SARA: Then what?

FRAN: I just have no goddamn idea where you're coming from. Like at all. I mean sure, dad isn't exactly the most emotionally available person but he worked his ass off to provide for us and now here we are and suddenly none of it is good enough for you.

SARA: Of course it's good enough.

FRAN: Then what?

SARA: After marrying your father it felt like I began relying on him for everything.

FRAN: That's such a crock. I mean it's not like you were some doting housewife. You had a career and a life.

SARA: I know. It's just somewhere along the line my life stopped feeling like it was mine, and that's the best way I can describe it. *(Beat)* Despite all this I do still think about him. What he's been doing with himself.

FRAN: He's opening a restaurant.

SARA: Up there?

FRAN: That's his plan.

SARA: That was originally my idea. Something we were going to do together.

FRAN: Tell me about this place you're moving into.

SARA: It's nice. Good windows. Close to campus.

FRAN: Joel mentioned you're teaching fewer courses.

SARA: I'm trying to focus on other things.

FRAN: Like your boyfriend?

SARA: My writing. Besides, Willias left.

FRAN: What?

SARA: He moved back to Georgia.

FRAN: I thought he was from Greece?

SARA: He's from Atlanta.

FRAN: Okay I'm really confused. Did you two break up?

SARA: Honestly, we were never actually together.

(JOEL *enters with wine glass full of water.*)

JOEL: Sorry I took so long. All I could find was an old wine glass in the dining room.

(JOEL *sees* FRAN's *facial expression.*)

JOEL: What?

FRAN: Did you know Willias is gone?

SARA: Fran.

JOEL: What?

FRAN: And that they weren't together?

JOEL: What?

SARA: Fran!

JOEL: What do you mean?

FRAN: They were never together.

JOEL: What are you talking about? What is Fran talking about??

SARA: Okay just both of you stop. You're giving me a headache.

JOEL: You were never with Willias?

SARA: He was a friend.

JOEL: A friend?

SARA: A good one. He supported me emotionally. Helped me believe that I could stand on my own.

JOEL: So if you weren't with him then why did you leave dad?

SARA: I just needed to be on my own. People look at me again. They see me as a living, breathing, sexual person. An individual. I've never truly felt what it's like to be on my own. It's wonderful and frightening. There's nothing more invigorating.

(A pause)

JOEL: I'm going to leave.

(JOEL turns and exits. After a moment he reenters, goes to the box of plates and glasses and kicks it violently several times. Tons of stuff breaks and shatters. He collects himself.)

JOEL: Now I'm leaving. *(He exits.)*

SARA: I never liked those plates anyway.

(The attempt at humor falls flat, as FRAN just stares at SARA.)

FRAN: You really did all this just so you could be on your own?

SARA: Yes.

FRAN: I guess you got your wish. *(She exits.)*

SARA: Fran. Fran!

(SARA gets up. After a moment she looks dizzy. She takes a sip of water, then drops the glass and falls down, passing out. FRAN enters.)

FRAN: Mom? *(She sees* SARA *on the ground.)* Mom!

*(*FRAN *runs to* SARA. *Lights fade.)*

Scene 9

(The next day. JOEL*'s studio. The goat statue is on the ground.* FRAN *enters. She goes to the statue and looks at it.* JOEL *enters from behind. He watches her a moment.)*

JOEL: I didn't hear you come in.

*(*FRAN *turns.)*

FRAN: The front was locked so I came in the back. *(Re: the statue)* One of your new ones?

JOEL: What do you think?

FRAN: Interesting. Though I'm not really into goats.

JOEL: Look, if you came to guilt me into going to see mom I already went.

FRAN: I know. The nurse told me. Though she said you didn't stay long.

JOEL: I was tired.

FRAN: I stopped by your place before coming here and James was on his way to airport. He said he hasn't seen you in over a week. Are you two not together anymore?

JOEL: I don't see how that's any of your business.

FRAN: I get that things are really crazy right now, but don't blow up the good in your life because you're pissed off.

JOEL: Suddenly she cares.

FRAN: I've always cared.

JOEL: For the past thirty years you haven't cared about anyone other than yourself. But now that mom's in the hospital you suddenly feel the need to be the glue.

FRAN: I didn't come to fight with you.

JOEL: So why did you? To let me know what an asshole I am? Or was it to assure me that everything is going to be alright? Maybe you came to buy some of my art that no one wants.

FRAN: Joel—

JOEL: I'm afraid you can't have the goat dog because mom already bought it out of pity. But I've got loads of other stuff. There's a sculpture of a monkey hawk.

FRAN: Joel.

JOEL: Over there is a kangaroo shark. If you commission me I can even make a snake horse.

FRAN: I came to give you this. *(She pulls out a card.)*

JOEL: What's that?

FRAN: The business card for the curator of James' show.

JOEL: And you're giving it to me why?

FRAN: James sent her images of your work and I guess she's interested. So you should call her.

JOEL: No thanks.

FRAN: Why not?

JOEL: It's table scraps!!

FRAN: What does that even mean?

JOEL: I don't know Fran. What does it mean?

FRAN: I don't know that's why I'm asking.

JOEL: I'm the better artist!! And I don't mean that in a subjective way. My art is literally better than his because it's more interesting and it's actually crafted, whereas all he does is throw shit on a canvass, sometimes literally, and no offense to you and dad, but his brand is just about pissing off republicans which is really a wow! So fucking original to take a pop shot at the societal hierarchy, which also ironically happens to be me because at my core I'm not an really artist am I? I'm just a thirty something trust fund baby living off my privilege. There it is! The truth has been revealed! And another thing—I'm so sick of everyone always feeling the need to look after me like I'm some kind of a helpless cripple. I mean what? Do I have a neon sign hovering over my head that reads charity case???

FRAN: People try to help you because they love you.

JOEL: Well I don't want or need anyone's help!! *(He rips up the card and throws it on the ground.)*

FRAN: Fine. Then go off and be miserable by yourself forever.

JOEL: But isn't that the point of all this? That we're destined to be alone and miserable? I mean look at dad. Look at mom. Look at you. You try so hard to cover up the shit storm your life has become with Chris. But everyone can see it.

FRAN: You don't know what you're talking about.

JOEL: We all know what he does, Fran. How he cheats on you. Sometimes he doesn't even come home, does he? And the worst part is that you let that bastard get away with it.

FRAN: Shut up.

JOEL: I mean dad tolerated the things he did for us, but why do you do what you do? Is it because you're weak? Because you're scared?

FRAN: I said shut up.

JOEL: Jesus. You're the most pathetic one out of all of us.

FRAN: You are so mentally fucked, Joel. I mean seriously.

JOEL: GET OUT OF MY STUDIO.

(FRAN *quickly exits the opposite way she originally entered. After a moment she returns.*)

FRAN: Jesus Christ I can't get the front door unlocked.

JOEL: Just go out the back!

(FRAN *exits the way she originally entered.*)

Scene 10

(*The next day. Hospital room.* SARA *is asleep in a bed.* FRAN *is sitting nearby, waiting, wearing the same clothes from the day before. She looks exhausted. Her phone rings. She looks at it, doesn't recognize the number, lets it ring a few times, then answers.*)

FRAN: Hello? I'm sorry who is this? (*We see on her face who it is. After a moment of listening—*) Don't ever call me again.

(FRAN *hangs up, trembling, exhales long and slow, maybe a tear rolls down her cheek but she wipes it away.*)

(*After a moment a* DOCTOR *enters.*)

DOCTOR: Hi excuse me.

FRAN: (*Wiping away another tear*) Yes.

DOCTOR: Sorry am I interrupting?

FRAN: (*Covering*) No. You're fine. Just have something in my eye.

DOCTOR: Still sleeping, huh?

FRAN: The past day she's been awake maybe thirty minutes.

DOCTOR: We haven't met yet. I'm Doctor Stevens.

FRAN: Nice to meet you. Fran, the daughter.

DOCTOR: So when your mom wakes, I should talk to her.

FRAN: Okay. Or you can talk to me and save yourself the return trip. I've got medical power of attorney.

(Beat)

DOCTOR: There are still treatment options available. But given her labs and the swelling of her lymph nodes and liver, we're looking at stage four.

FRAN: Stage four?

DOCTOR: Leukemia.

(As lights transition they speak a moment mutedly, then DOCTOR *exits.)*

(Time passes. FRAN *gets up, dazed and goes and sits in the hall. We still see* SARA *asleep in her bed.)*

*(*JOEL *enters the hallway with two paper cups of coffee. After a moment.)*

JOEL: Those the same clothes from yesterday?

FRAN: They are.

JOEL: Want one? It's Vending machine coffee. Tastes like shit but it's caffeine.

*(*JOEL *hands* FRAN *a cup and she takes a sip. He sits down next to her.)*

JOEL: About yesterday. I said some really stupid things and I'm an idiot.

FRAN: I'm just happy to see you.

JOEL: How is she?

FRAN: Sleeping.

JOEL: Dad know about any of this?

FRAN: Not yet.

JOEL: Probably for the best. *(Beat)* You've showed a lot of composure lately. In that way you take after dad. He always paid more attention to you. He even coached your little league team. For an entire summer he took you out into the back yard every single day and tried to teach you how to throw a baseball. After all that practice, how could you not throw a ball more than five feet? *(Beat)* After you left yesterday I called that curator. She bought five sculptures over the phone.

FRAN: Really?

JOEL: She called my work "existentially provocative".

FRAN: Go to Paris.

JOEL: What?

FRAN: Get on a plane tonight. Go to James' show and be there for him.

JOEL: But with mom in the hospital—

FRAN: Joel listen to me. Go to Paris. I will hold down the fort.

(Beat)

JOEL: Okay. I owe you one. *(Beat)* Sitting here, it really puts it all in perspective. I mean you think you're suffering and then you come to a place like this. *(Beat)* I had this dream last night. I was a kid again. It was summer up at the lake. I was swimming. I turned back to shore and it was so far away. I started to swim towards it, but it just kept getting further away. Then I couldn't see shore at all. Just water. *(Beat)* I guess I should go in. See mom before I jet off. *(He starts to get up.)*

FRAN: Joel. Can you sit with me a little while longer?

JOEL: Is there something you're not telling me?

FRAN: I'm just really, tired.

(JOEL *sits back down. He and* FRAN *sit in silence. In the transition light we see* JOEL *get up, visit* SARA *then exit. After a moment* FRAN *gets up and goes into the room.*)

Scene 11

(The next day. The hospital room. SARA *is now awake.)*

FRAN: How do you feel?

SARA: Groggy. You look like shit.

FRAN: Thanks.

SARA: It's an observation not a criticism. Is Joel here?

FRAN: He's on his way to Paris.

SARA: What?

FRAN: He sold some work to the curator of James' show.

SARA: We should go.

FRAN: Where?

SARA: To Paris!

FRAN: Okay mom?

SARA: I've never been and I've always wanted to go. The shopping, the architecture, the croissants. We could even get matching berets and go to The Louvre!

FRAN: Mom I know.

SARA: Know what?

FRAN: You're sick.

SARA: Don't be overly worried about my passing out. It's just because I'm not eating much and with all the stress of—

FRAN: Mom.

(Beat)

SARA: How'd you find out?

FRAN: One of your doctors told me.

SARA: That's confidential.

FRAN: You were asleep and I have your power of attorney.

SARA: I thought I'd changed that to James.

FRAN: Why didn't you tell us?

SARA: It wasn't anyone's business.

FRAN: Are you fucking kidding me?

SARA: I was managing it. At first even beating it. Then I wasn't.

FRAN: So that's why you left dad? Why you've been doing anything you want?

SARA: Is it wrong to live how I've always wanted?

FRAN: When it hurts the people who love you? Yes.

SARA: Great. I'm the villain. Again.

FRAN: That's not what I said.

SARA: It's what you implied and I'm sick of it. Sick of feeling obligated. Sick of doing things because it's what people think I should be doing, and then when I don't do them I get attacked and criticized.

FRAN: When has that ever happened?

SARA: It's happening right now! Does anyone else know about this? Joel?

FRAN: If I'd told him he wouldn't have left.

SARA: And your father?

FRAN: No.

SARA: Good. Keep it that way.

FRAN: I think he's got a right to know.

SARA: So he can hold it over my fucking head?

FRAN: He loves you.

SARA: Oh so that's why he's having the house torn down.

FRAN: You're the one who imploded a marriage to fulfill a fantasy.

SARA: Fantasy?? I'm dying! *(Beat)* I bet you're loving this, aren't you? Your cold-hearted selfish bitch of mother is wasting away, and you've got a front row seat.

FRAN: I want to help you.

SARA: I don't need help! Now get out. GET THE HELL OUT OF HERE!!!!

(FRAN starts to leave. She stops. After a moment she goes back to SARA. FRAN holds out her hand. SARA takes it.)

(In transition SARA exits. FRAN stands alone. Her phone rings. She looks at it, prepares herself and then answers.)

FRAN: *(Calm but we can tell she's trembling on the inside.)* I don't want to talk but I want you to know that she called and told me what's happened and fuck you but also fuck me for knowing something was going on and pretending it wasn't. All your stuff needs to be out of the house by tomorrow, goodbye. *(She hangs up. Exhales and exits.)*

Scene 12

(A few days later. Inside an old barn. JOHN enters wearing a vest and beanie hat and boots. FRAN enters, wearing a jacket and a scarf.)

JOHN: You came on the right weekend. The snow just started falling. The way the white drapes over everything makes the landscape round and soft. It's like a painting out there.

FRAN: It's freezing and wet.

JOHN: Exposure to the elements gets you in tune with your basic self. Anyway, here we are.

FRAN: Where?

JOHN: My new restaurant!

FRAN: This is an abandoned barn.

JOHN: Before you go trying to convince me how bad of an idea this is let me explain the layout. Where we're standing is going to be the entry. And there'll be a door right behind you.

FRAN: That's a wall.

JOHN: Use your imagination. And over there's going to be the seating area. And the kitchen will be over there- grill top, deep fryer, two fridges at least. With some careful design I can even have a walk in freezer. And over there a window with a neon sign— "John's Kitchen Counter".

FRAN: Dad you need to come home.

JOHN: Home is getting torn down next week.

FRAN: I meant for you to return to the city.

JOHN: Why would I do that?

FRAN: Because Mom needs you.

JOHN: Where's her poet?

FRAN: Gone.

JOHN: I told her that would happen. But did she listen? No. She was too busy having her little sex-capade.

FRAN: They weren't together like that. It turns out they were just friends.

JOHN: I'm not going back.

FRAN: Dad.

JOHN: I'm entering a new chapter.

FRAN: She's sick. Cancer.

JOHN: Why didn't you tell me sooner?

FRAN: I'm telling you now.

JOHN: For Christ sakes we just sat in the damn car for twenty minutes.

FRAN: I didn't know how to bring it up.

JOHN: She in the hospital?

FRAN: She's at Joel's.

JOHN: He doesn't have a spare bedroom.

FRAN: He went to Paris.

JOHN: I thought James went to Paris.

FRAN: It's a long story. And I'll tell you all about it on the way back home.

JOHN: Even if I went back, what would I say? "Hi. Haven't seen you in over six months. Sorry you have cancer." It's absurd.

FRAN: Dad she's dying.

(Pause)

JOHN: I need to get back to the cabin.

FRAN: Dad.

JOHN: It's gonna be dark soon and I'd like to get a fire started.

FRAN: Quite a reaction.

JOHN: How am I supposed to react?

FRAN: How about with a little compassion.

JOHN: So now I'm supposed to give her compassion. After the way she shit on me.

FRAN: You're not innocent in this either.

JOHN: What does that mean?

FRAN: You're stubborn, and hard headed. You ignored the fact that mom was desperately unhappy and had us all carry on like we were some normal family.

JOHN: We were a normal family!

FRAN: Jesus dad.

JOHN: So I'm the one who ruined the marriage? I'm the one who destroyed everything? I suppose I'm the one who gave your mom cancer?!

FRAN: Dad—

JOHN: Why is it always me who's doing everything wrong? Why doesn't anyone else get scrutinized?!

FRAN: You're miserable and lonely.

JOHN: Of course I am!

FRAN: So do something about it!

JOHN: WHAT AM I SUPPOSED TO DO?

FRAN: STOP PRETENDING YOU'RE OKAY.

JOHN: WE'RE ALL PRETENDING!!!

(Beat)

FRAN: I left Chris.

JOHN: What?

FRAN: I kicked him out. Changed the locks. The whole deal.

JOHN: I thought you two were okay.

FRAN: He got back with the stewardess. Got her pregnant.

JOHN: Jesus Fran.

FRAN: I think I put up with Chris' shit for so long because I was scared of being alone. But when I was with him I never felt more alone.

JOHN: You want me to beat the shit out of him?

FRAN: You couldn't.

JOHN: I can hire someone.

FRAN: Tempting.

(FRAN *and* JOHN *hug.*)

JOHN: How the hell did we get here? Things weren't supposed to be like this.

FRAN: Shit happens. Whether or not we want to deal with it is up to us.

(JOHN *looks around the space.*)

JOHN: In one week it will be the shortest day of the year. I'd hoped to be open by June. *(Beat)* Get the car started. I'll lock up.

(FRAN *exits.* JOHN *pauses a moment. Then he exits.*)

Scene 13

(*Early the following spring.* JOHN *is sitting on the pier fishing next to* SARA, *who is reading a paper.* JOEL, *wearing sunglasses and covered with a blanket, is sitting next to them.* JOHN *is wearing his flannel shirt.* SARA *is wearing a light vest and a head wrap.*)

SARA: Good tidings abound. Be weary of murky opportunities. A fortune easily gained is easily lost. Love is on the rise.

(JOHN *looks towards* SARA.)

SARA: It's my horoscope.

JOHN: You always loved your horoscopes.

SARA: Would you like to hear yours?

JOHN: You know I don't believe in that stuff.

SARA: I think it relates to the day you're having.

JOHN: What kind of day is that?

SARA: Not catching any fish.

JOHN: It's still early.

SARA: You haven't gotten a single bite.

JOHN: And my horoscope's the culprit?

SARA: There are external factors beyond our control.

JOHN: Read it to me.

SARA: Persistence is a virtue. But today nothing will go correctly. Lay low.
The deck is stacked against you.

JOHN: Too bad you didn't read that to me earlier. I'd have just stayed in bed.

(JOEL *wakes up.*)

JOEL: What are you two talking about?

JOHN: Someone's finally awake.

JOEL: What time is it?

JOHN: Half past three.

JOEL: I can't remember the last time I was so relaxed. I could live out here.

SARA: I'd think living in a place with nothing to do would get boring.

JOHN: There's plenty to do. You can chop wood, go on hikes, garden.

SARA: You don't garden.

(FRAN *enters, wearing jeans and a sweatshirt.*)

JOHN: I was gonna start. For the restaurant.

FRAN: John's Kitchen Counter?

JOHN: Simple and to the point.

JOEL: For the record I liked the name. Sort of.

JOHN: It's not about the name. It's about the food.

FRAN: Dad I love you but opening a restaurant would've been a horrible mistake.

JOHN: I'm a business man. A restaurant is a business.

JOEL: Come on dad. Since you moved back you've been happier.

JOHN: It was an easy transition. And finding a place wasn't as hard as I thought.

SARA: You could have moved back into the house. I've only got one live-in nurse.

FRAN: It's probably for the best he didn't. Juanita is strange about men.

JOEL: It's her background. Cubans are very traditional about relationships.

FRAN: What?

JOEL: What? I know a lot about Cuban culture.

FRAN: Says the guy who at age eleven thought Cuba was a person who made pressed sandwiches.

JOEL: And you thought Mexico was a company that made tortillas.

FRAN: When I was six.

JOEL: You were seven.

JOHN: *(Sarcastic)* Gosh this has just been a lovely weekend hasn't it?

SARA: All we're missing is a box of smashed plates.

FRAN: Come on. It's been plenty fun. Just wish the weather would've cooperated more. It's May and I can still see my breath.

SARA: Actually we're lucky. This time of year it usually snows.

FRAN: No way.

SARA: It's true. We came up here for our honeymoon and got stuck in a blizzard.

JOHN: Just the two of us, a pack of hotdogs and a space heater.

JOEL: If that's not the portrait of romance I don't know what is.

JOHN: I'm sorry James couldn't make it up. This is a family occasion and at this point he's practically family.

JOEL: He wanted to come but he needed to get ready for his new show: *White People—The Modern Pandemic.*

JOHN: I'll be sure to see that one.

JOEL: Speaking of family occasions, where are we doing thanksgiving this year?

FRAN: Joel.

JOEL: I just think it's important to nail down a location that will accommodate us all.

SARA: We'll do it at the house like we always do.

JOEL: Actually I was thinking we could change it up. Maybe we could all come up here.

FRAN: Kinda a long drive. Plus the roads are always clogged that week.

JOEL: Then how about your place?

FRAN: My place?

JOEL: Your dining room is huge.

FRAN: How about your place?

JOEL: My place is tiny.

FRAN: You have better parking.

JOHN: How about we change the subject?

SARA: Great idea.

FRAN: What are we thinking for dinner?

JOHN: I was hoping for freshly caught fish.

SARA: Not looking good on that front.

JOEL: Maybe we can make tacos.

SARA: I think tacos sound great.

JOHN: Fran, make sure to get the lean ground beef and the crunchy shells. Also sour cream.

FRAN: Why are you telling me?

JOHN: Because you're going to the store.

FRAN: Why do I have to go?

JOHN: Because I said so.

FRAN: *(To* JOEL*)* Come with me.

JOEL: Why?

FRAN: I still get lost on the roads up here and you've got a good sense of direction.

JOEL: I'm relaxing.

FRAN: If you don't get your ass out of that chair you'll be relaxing in the lake.

(JOEL *slowly gets up.*)

JOEL: You two gonna be alright on your own?

JOHN: I think we'll manage.

FRAN: We should be back in thirty.

JOEL: If we're gone any longer call the police. *(Beat)* Seriously.

FRAN: See you soon mom.

(FRAN *goes over and kisses* SARA *on the forehead.* FRAN *and* JOEL *exit. A silent moment. Then* JOHN *exhales.*)

SARA: What are you thinking?

JOHN: Who says I am?

SARA: You exhaled.

JOHN: Guess I was thinking that this is like old times again. Except the kids seem happy. Fran especially.

SARA: She met someone.

JOHN: She didn't tell me.

SARA: She probably doesn't want to jinx it.

JOHN: Tell me about him.

SARA: His name is Denny. He's an accountant. Who rides a motorcycle.

JOHN: That's different.

SARA: She really likes him.

JOHN: Maybe some day we'll get to meet him.

SARA: I've never seen anything like it.

JOHN: What?

SARA: This fog.

JOHN: What fog?

SARA: The fog that's all around us.

JOHN: I don't see any fog.

SARA: It's everywhere. It's slowly covering the lake. Look. It's even starting to creep up the trees.

JOHN: Are you okay?

(*For a moment* SARA *braces herself and shakes. It looks like she's shivering.*)

JOHN: Sara? Sara?

(JOHN *grabs* SARA. *She snaps out of her spell.*)

SARA: What?

JOHN: You got pale and started shaking.

SARA: I'm fine. It was just a chill.

(Beat)

JOHN: It's because it rained earlier.

SARA: What?

JOHN: The fog.

SARA: You see it too?

JOHN: Yes.

SARA: I was thinking. Maybe you and I could stay up here for a little while longer.

JOHN: Really?

SARA: The kids drove their own cars.

JOHN: You've got your clinic appointment Monday.

SARA: I was thinking I might stop going.

JOHN: What?

SARA: It's not doing anything other than making me sicker than I already am. Plus that place gives me the creeps. Everything smells so, sterile. And no one smiles.

JOHN: What part of the week do you look forward to most?

SARA: When clinic is over.

JOHN: So if you stop going you'll lose your favorite part of the week.

SARA: I say this from a place of warmth. Blow me.

JOHN: You know I'm right.

SARA: *(Beat)* You look good.

JOHN: I've been exercising. Lost some weight.

SARA: I meant you seem brighter. More happy.

JOHN: I started seeing someone.

SARA: A woman?

JOHN: A therapist. And yes she is a woman.

SARA: How long have you been seeing her?

JOHN: Since I got back. It helps me cope with things. I feel silly telling you that.

SARA: Why?

JOHN: Don't want you to think I'm crazy.

SARA: I love you.

JOHN: Love you too.

SARA: No. I mean, I'm still in love with you. I think right now I love you more now than I've loved anything.

JOHN: Thank you for that.

SARA: Wow. That's embarrassing.

JOHN: Sara—

SARA: Just forget I said anything.

JOHN: I don't know what to say.

SARA: Why are you here? Do you pity me?

JOHN: Of course not.

SARA: Then it must be guilt. Now that I'm sick you feel you're somehow responsible?

JOHN: Can we have a conversation where everything doesn't jump to extremes?

(SARA *gets up.*)

JOHN: Where are you going?

SARA: Back to the cabin.

(JOHN *gets up.*)

JOHN: You can't walk that far by yourself.

SARA: Then I'll crawl.

JOHN: You're not crawling up a hill.

SARA: I'm damn well going to try.

JOHN: For the love of GOD sit down!!

(SARA *is caught off guard by* JOHN's *tone. She sits. A silent moment.*)

SARA: I want to apologize to you.

JOHN: For what?

SARA: Everything.

JOHN: Sometimes I feel like I coerced you into marrying me.

SARA: What?

JOHN: That's one of the things I talk about with my therapist. I remember the first time I ever saw you. That party. You were on the porch wearing this yellow dress. I walked up to you and without saying anything I tried to kiss you. Then I got punched. By your boyfriend who was standing next to you.

SARA: You were very passionate.

JOHN: I was quite drunk.

SARA: It was more than that. You had this look in your eye. Like you saw something you wanted and nothing would stop you from getting it. You didn't have any fear. You weren't scared to fight for what you wanted.

JOHN: When you're young you can afford to be reckless.

SARA: Stop being so damn afraid! I've wasted so much time being afraid. Don't make my mistake. Let go and take a risk. Fulfil you wildest desire.

JOHN: Sara—

SARA: If there's one thing I know about you, it's that you don't like to admit when problems exist. You ignore problems because you want everyone to be happy. But other people's happiness is up to them, not you. Stop being so stoic. Stop hiding behind your veil of polite-ness. Even right now. You should hate me! I destroyed everything we had.

JOHN: That's not true. The house is still standing. Also, I never signed them.

SARA: What?

JOHN: The divorce papers.

SARA: Of course you did. Didn't you?

JOHN: I burned them.

SARA: You burned them?

JOHN: When I was living up here. One night I made a fire, tossed them in, and that was that.

SARA: So you mean to tell me we're still—

JOHN: Uh huh.

SARA: Huh. Do the kids know?

JOHN: I haven't told them.

SARA: Do you think we should?

JOHN: Do you?

SARA: It might make things weird.

JOHN: Agreed.

SARA: Why didn't you sign them?

JOHN: Why do you think?

SARA: I'd like to hear you to say it.

JOHN: Do you really need me to?

SARA: Yes.

JOHN: Alright. *(Beat)* Sara? You can be a real bitch.

SARA: Well. Forget about getting laid.

(JOHN *starts to laugh.* SARA *joins in. Her laugh turns into a coughing fit. It gets dangerous.)*

JOHN: Look at me. Little breaths. Little breaths.

(SARA *gets it under control.)*

SARA: My lungs feel like they're on fire.

JOHN: You just need to rest.

SARA: What I need is to get it over with. I can barely walk, my bones ache, my mouth is constantly dry. My insides feel mushy.

JOHN: We can talk to your doctors.

SARA: Yesterday something happened.

JOHN: What?

SARA: I was sitting out back reading. I looked up and saw a man standing at the edge of the pines watching me. At first I didn't recognize him, but then I knew who he was.

JOHN: Who?

SARA: Your father.

JOHN: My father's been dead ten years.

SARA: Which is why it scared me. But the more I looked at him the less frightened I became. Until everything in me was just, calm. Then he turned and went into the woods. *(Beat)* What do you think of that?

JOHN: I think you've always had an active imagination.

SARA: I didn't imagine it.

JOHN: People see things that aren't there all the—

SARA: He's here for me. I can feel it.

JOHN: What are you telling me?

SARA: That everything is okay.

(*Pause*)

JOHN: We should go in.

SARA: I know. But can we sit here a little longer?

(*Beat*)

JOHN: Yes.

(JOHN *and* SARA *sit in silence. After a moment*)

JOHN: Do you hear that?

SARA: What?

JOHN: The cry of a loon. It sounds like it's coming from the other side of the lake.

(*After a moment* SARA *takes* JOHN's *hand.*)

SARA: John—

JOHN: Shh. There it is again.

(JOHN *and* SARA *sit in silence as the lights slowly fade.*)

END OF PLAY